THE WONDER
OF THE
CHRISTIAN STORY

Other works by Elizabeth Wang also published by Radiant Light:

Teachings-in-Prayer Volume One: Spiritual Training.
Teachings-in-Prayer Volume Two: Spiritual Nourishment.
Teachings-in-Prayer Volume Three: Spiritual Work.
Teachings-in-Prayer Volume Four: Spiritual Life.
Teachings-in-Prayer Volume Five: Spiritual Peace.
Living and Working for the King of Kings, Christ.
"My Priests are Sacred."
How to Pray (Part One: Foundations)
How to Pray Part Two: Liturgy and Morals.
Falling in Love: A Spiritual Autobiography.
Radiant Light: How the Work Began.
"Speak about Hope."
"Speak about Holiness."
An Invitation from Christ: prayer card.
A message from the Father: prayer card.
The Holy Sacrifice of the Mass: Mass Poster.
Radiant Light Conference Video 1999.
Radiant Light Conference Video 2000.
The Christian Story Video.
What is Jesus like?
What is Mary like?
The Majesty of the Mass.
The Beauty of the Rosary.
The Glory of the Holy Trinity.
Prayer Postcards: Hope and encouragement.

Radiant Light *books, paintings and posters are available to buy in person or by mail-order from:*

St Pauls (By Westminster Cathedral)
Morpeth Terrace, Victoria, London SW1P 1EP, UK.
Tel: 020-7828-5582; Fax: 020-7828-3329
email: bookshop@Stpauls.org.uk.
Visit the Radiant Light web-site for an updated catalogue:
www.radiantlight.org.uk

THE WONDER
OF THE
CHRISTIAN STORY

WRITTEN AND ILLUSTRATED BY
ELIZABETH WANG

This book is published by **Radiant Light**
25 Rothamsted Avenue
Harpenden, Herts., AL5 2DN, UK

First published February 2002

'C.C.C.' refers to the '*Catechism of the Catholic Church*',
Geoffrey Chapman, London 1994, copyright © 1994
Geoffrey Chapman - Libreria Editrice Vaticana

Scripture quotations have been taken from the Jerusalem Bible
published and copyright 1966, 1967 and 1968
by Darton, Longman and Todd Ltd
and Doubleday & Co. Inc.

Text and illustrations by Elizabeth Wang

Text and illustrations copyright © Radiant Light 2002

Front cover design: detail from oil painting:
"Christ is our Bridge"
OIL:M-81
by Elizabeth Wang

ISBN 1-902960-38-6

"Why, Yahweh, leave us to stray from your ways
and harden our hearts against fearing you?
Return, for the sake of your servants,
the tribes of your inheritance.
Why have the wicked set foot in your sanctuary,
why are our enemies trampling your sanctuary?
We have long been like people you do not rule,
people who do not bear your name.
Oh, that you would tear the heavens open
and come down ..."

(Is: 63:17-20)

CONTENTS

INTRODUCTION.

The paintings in this book were all exhibited in the Conference Rooms at St. Paul's Bookshop, next to Westminster Cathedral, in August 2001. A taped commentary was available at the time; and that same commentary, with the images, is available today both on video and in the following pages. So I haven't set out to provide a text book for catechesis; rather, I've just shared my thoughts about my paintings: about the truths they show out, and about the wonderful nature of God Who has reached out through His Son, Jesus Christ, to change and transform us by the power of His Spirit.

Our lives can be marvellously changed when we really believe that we are loved by God, and that our sins can be forgiven. We can find joy and security through the sacraments of the Church; and then, in the friendship of Christ, we can begin to share our love and joy with other people, and to spread the Good News; and we can even dare to believe that, by God's grace, we can achieve holiness, and reach Heaven. There, we can enjoy His marvellous presence forever, in the company of all the Saints and holy Angels; and so I urge everyone who opens this book to turn to Christ in prayer, and also to find out more about Him - and the Father and the Holy Spirit - through the sure teaching of the Catholic Church.

Elizabeth Wang
6 January 2002
Feast of the Epiphany

PART ONE

A BRIEF HISTORY
OF SALVATION

1

TWO 'ARMS' FROM THE FATHER.

The Word and the Spirit are like two arms from the Father.

On the left is Christ the Son of God as He descends to earth to live amongst us and to die for us; and on the right is the Holy Spirit, represented by the wing of a dove: the Spirit sent by Christ from the Father.

It's as if God our Father, in Heaven, has sent out rays of glory to illuminate our lives on earth; almost as though, through Christ and the Spirit, He reaches out two arms to enfold all humanity in His embrace.

He didn't send Christ His Son to earth without first preparing a People to receive Him; and so, through Patriarchs and Prophets, the Father caused human hearts to yearn for holiness - and promised to send a Saviour who would bring us deliverance from sin and darkness.

Christ, the Word of God, took flesh from Mary just over two thousand years ago. He became man, for our sakes. And after His death on the Cross for our sins, and His Resurrection, by which He opened Heaven's 'door', He sent the Holy Spirit from the Father to give Divine life to all who would accept it.

All who live on earth are touched - whether or not they know it - by the powerful and loving actions of the Holy Trinity. Father, Son and Holy Spirit are One God: holy and transcendent yet lovingly holding all Creation in existence.

TWO 'ARMS' FROM THE FATHER
(OIL-M:1439)

2

THE WORD LEAPED DOWN.

Christ came down from Heaven on a great flood
of the Spirit's grace and love and power.

When Christ came down from Heaven to become man, it was as
though He leaped down, joyfully. It was as if a great flood of the
Spirit's grace and love and power poured out through the bars of
Heaven as Christ stripped Himself of glory at His Incarnation.

Christ came in weakness, as a little child; and His purpose was to save
from Eternal death all who would believe in Him. He is truly a man
Who in His earthly life was sometimes hungry and thirsty, lonely and
heartbroken. Yet He isn't merely a man. He isn't someone who
simply developed a longing in adult life to speak about a Kingdom of
justice and peace but was unaware of the consequences of His
preaching.

For the whole of His life on earth, Christ was aware of His Divine
Origin, His mission and purpose, the manner of His death, and the
glorious fulfilment which lay ahead through His Resurrection and
Ascension; and He was glad to be able to offer hope and love and
peace to His sinful and helpless brothers and sisters.

THE WORD LEAPED DOWN
(OIL-M:1320)

5

3

THE INCARNATION.

God the Son was made flesh in the womb
of the Blessed Virgin Mary.

We know, from the Sacred Tradition of the Church and from Holy Scripture, that the Holy Trinity was at work at a certain moment of history to effect a wonderful event. By Divine power, God the Holy Spirit fulfilled God the Father's plan by causing God the Son to be 'made flesh' in the Virgin Mary's womb, at her consent. Jesus was going to live and die amongst us, true God and true man.

As an infant, Jesus was taught, guarded and guided by Mary; and she had been well-prepared for her task. On the one hand, she is a normal human being who has experienced deep emotions, and made painful choices; on the other hand she was long ago chosen and prepared by God to be a uniquely-holy human person.

Unlike us, she was conceived free from Original Sin. She was kept free, because God allowed her to benefit, in advance, from the saving death her son would undergo; and so she was worthy to become the Virgin 'Mother of God'. She cared devotedly for Jesus in His childhood, with St. Joseph's help; and then when her son reached maturity, she was one with Him in heart and mind and spirit, both in the joys of His ministry and in His times of utter desolation.

THE INCARNATION
(OIL-M:1349)

7

4

THE VISITATION.

Mary and Elizabeth knew that the whole world
would benefit from the work of their sons.

Mary and Elizabeth are standing side by side, thinking about their unborn children, and looking out, as it were, upon the whole world.

When Mary was visited, earlier, by the Angel Gabriel, she listened carefully, and then consented to God's plan; and that's why she conceived Christ in her womb, by the Spirit's power; but she longed to share her joy, and that's why she travelled South to spend some time with Elizabeth, a close relation who was also pregnant.

Elizabeth recognised that Mary had been chosen to be the Mother of the Lord; and we can suppose that Mary knew that Elizabeth's son would have a special role. He would eventually be known as 'John the Baptiser' and would prepare the way for Jesus, just before Jesus set out to preach and teach and heal in adult life. Mary knew that the whole world would one day be affected by the work and witness of their two sons.

Mary remained full of love for God, and full of gratitude for her privileged role - especially when she saw Christ set out, in adult life, to preach, teach, heal and comfort so many people. She was His most devoted follower, as she watched this living embodiment of Divine love and compassion reach out to the sick and the sinful who flocked around Him. She followed in His footsteps when the adulation turned to envy and hatred; and she trusted in Him, and waited patiently beneath the Cross when He allowed Himself to be seized and put to death in order to fulfil His mission on earth.

THE VISITATION
(OIL-M:1714)

9

5

CHRIST OUR BROTHER.

*Christ the God-man offered His life in sacrifice,
praying for sinners to be forgiven.*

Although Christ is a Divine Person He made Himself our true brother when He became man, flesh and blood like us, when He was born on earth just over two thousand years ago. In His earthly life, Christ the God-man treasured all sorts of earthly joys and good friendships; yet He was physically weak like us, in that He suffered, was hungry, and needed sleep. When He was struck, He bled, like us; and when He was crucified, He died on the Cross: the most loveable and loving Person Who has ever lived on earth; yet since He's a Divine Person Who has two natures - a Divine nature and a human nature - He is well qualified to act as the Mediator between Mankind and the Godhead.

Here we see Christ as he suffers and dies on the Cross, offering His life in sacrifice, praying for sinners to be forgiven. He is sinless, yet He prayed as a spokesman for all humanity: for people everywhere who had become separated from God the Father.

And just as He prayed for us from the Cross, during His Passion, that's what He does today, at every Mass, when He is Really Present amongst us after the Consecration, though 'disguised' under the appearance of bread and wine.

Wherever Christ is sacramentally Present, He is praying to His Father, on our behalf, asking for our sins to be forgiven, and for all sorts of blessings and graces to be poured down upon us. As St Paul says (Ro 8:34), Christ is ever living to intercede for us; so we know that Christ prays for us both in Heaven and in our sanctuary.

CHRIST OUR BROTHER
(OIL-M:1351B)

11

6

THE BRIDGE TO HEAVEN.

*By His obedience, Christ has bridged the gulf
between earth and Heaven.*

Christ is the 'bridge' between earth and Heaven. He Himself is the way back to God the Father; that's what He's told us, through the Gospels. All who put their trust in Him, and share His life, and try to live as He lived, in truth and holiness, and joy and loving kindness, have a sure hope of crossing that bridge one day, at death, to enter the beauty and peace of Heaven.

Christ is God and man; and during His earthly life, Christ accepted the consequences of living amongst sinful people. He accepted the mockery which is almost inevitable when someone pure hearted speaks the truth about God's holiness and about human weakness.

When He was arrested and tormented Christ didn't retaliate with hatred, but willingly offered His life as a sacrifice for sin. He prayed for us all, from the Cross. He died in torment, because in His human nature He was a frail human being like ourselves - though sinless; yet being God as well as man He knew that death couldn't hold Him.

Just as He had predicted, Christ broke through death and rose from the grave to a new, indestructible life. It was through first dying, and then rising and entering Heaven, that He bridged the gulf between earth and heaven: a gulf which had appeared when human beings first rebelled against God, to live in pride and disobedience.

THE BRIDGE TO HEAVEN
(OIL-M:81)

13

7

THE RESURRECTION.

*Christ came out of the tomb, to the fierce joy,
relief and amazement of His friends.*

Christ rose from the dead on the third day, just as He had predicted. Though He had suffered and died as other men do, and had been buried by His sorrowful friends, death couldn't 'hold' Him, because He is God as well as man; and so He came out of the tomb.

Which of us can imagine the fierce joy, relief, and amazement of Jesus' close friends all those centuries ago? The wonderful man they'd seen dead and buried was now alive again. They had seen His beloved face, and heard Him speaking to them tenderly once more.

We've only to read the letters of St. Paul and some of the other Apostles, to realise that the joy and exhilaration of Christ's friends was to last all their lives. For years to come, they gloried in the knowledge of Jesus' nearness, and remained on fire with gratitude that He had been raised up to a new life in which they hoped to share when their work on earth was ended. Yet they understand the full significance of Christ's Resurrection. It was more than the restoration to them, by an extraordinary power, of a beloved friend. It was the proof that evil cannot overcome good. It was the vindication of Christ's words and witness. It was the fulfilment of His promise. It was the fulfilment of the hope held out to their ancestors: that God would raise up a Saviour from amongst them. It was the triumph of the Father's plan.

THE RESURRECTION
(OIL-M:1084C)

15

8

CHRIST, AT HEAVEN'S DOOR.

Only through Christ can we be brought to Heaven, at
death, to share His glory and to see the Father's face.

At His Ascension Christ greets His Father, Who holds open the door
of Heaven not only for Christ, but also for the thousands of Christ's
faithful friends of future ages who will love Christ and put their trust
in Him.

Christ has been raised up, by the Spirit's power, to a new and glorious
life; and this means that He will never die again; and He has promised
that whoever belongs to Him and remains faithful can share His life
of joy for all Eternity, in Heaven - which He entered some weeks after
His Resurrection, when He had finished instructing His disciples.

We have been given the hope of Eternal happiness only because of
Christ's suffering, death, Resurrection and Ascension.

During His life on earth, Christ urged people all over the country to
put their trust in Him and to follow His Way. He knew that when He
had completed His saving work on earth He would enter Heaven,
reuniting Mankind with the Godhead; and He shared the good news
that His faithful friends are brought 'high', at death, to share His glory
and to see the Father's face.

CHRIST, AT HEAVEN'S DOOR
(OIL-M:1588)

9

FIRE FROM HEAVEN.

The Holy Spirit is like fire from Heaven, bringing
His love, purity, wisdom and power.

If we give our consent to Him, the Holy Spirit acts upon us to work a marvellous transformation. He is like a fire from Heaven: a Divine and powerful Fire which brings light to our souls. He also scorches by His radiance; He can scour, burnish and beautify us. He inspires, consoles, and enlivens us; and He can make us pure and strong.

Jesus once said that He had come to cast fire upon the earth, and that He was longing for the world to be ablaze. He meant - on fire with His Spirit's love.

Christ sent His Spirit from the Father first to those who were waiting in the Upper Room, at Pentecost, and then to every generation of believers; and by that same Spirit God our Father can purify our souls in prayer, give perfect light and joy to our inmost hearts, demonstrate His love, share His life to a greater degree, teach us something about His nature, and even draw us to rest within His heart in contemplation.

It is the Holy Spirit who causes faithful souls to glimpse Divine love in its beauty and perfection. He enables us to see that Divine love is unchanging yet alive. It is a powerful love which is warm and effective. This is a love which consists of gentleness and peace as well as infinite power and majesty.

FIRE FROM HEAVEN
(OIL-M:1941)

10

A CORNER OF THE KINGDOM.

*A corner of the Kingdom is established on earth wherever
people offer their lives in God's service, for God's glory.*

The Church which Christ has founded is like a Kingdom of Light: or
like a garden, of which a little corner can be seen on earth: a garden
brilliantly-lit by the radiant glory of God. Yet the Church is greater
than the visible Church on earth. The rest of the Kingdom stretches
up towards Heaven, where it is populated by the Saints and the Holy
Angels, and, close by, those people who have died 'in Christ' but who
are in need of purification - the holy souls of Purgatory.

In every part of the Kingdom, God reigns, in His Infinite glory and
love; yet the small area which can be seen on earth is a place made
holy through Christ. Everyone who lives there can experience an
extraordinary sort of joy, and a sense of safety in spiritual matters - in
a way unknown to those who live in spiritual darkness.

The good news is that everyone who believes in Christ can receive the
Holy Spirit through Baptism and become a full member of the Church
through Baptism, Confirmation and Eucharist. Through praying
within the Church, each soul who is now forgiven, reconciled, taught
and fed by Christ, and who strives to do His Will, is a true child of
God and of His Kingdom.

A CORNER OF THE KINGDOM
(OIL-M:1332)

21

11

THE SACRED TRADITION.

Christ's followers are making a way through life's 'rough ground,' so that other people can walk in the Sacred Tradition which leads to God.

Here in the wilderness is a road which is still under construction. The thousands of people on the completed section move forward with confidence, however, guided by the 'shepherds' placed by Christ at the head of the column; and those 'shepherds' and teachers are the Bishops and other members of the Clergy, who hold aloft the Sacred Scriptures.

This road is like the Sacred Tradition. It is the Way of God's own People: those who belong to Christ's Church. This is the safe road which leads to the Father.

Within the Church, the Sacred Tradition is not something dead, but alive. It is something perpetually new, or perpetually expanding - like a firm road which is being built upon rough ground after careful preparation; and the Bishops who are united in faith and government and worship lead the whole community of believers to work as one. Together, everyone marks and makes plain the direction of the road at each moment; and they excavate the roadway in obedience to Christ's plan.

The people put down hard-core, and use staves to pack down the layers beneath the surface; and the layers represent the works, inspirations, prayers and virtues of the Saints of each age; and then God's People put in place the firm surface on which God invites everyone to walk. The durable and trustworthy surface represents the united witness, in each era, of all true and holy believers - the greatest and the least - who are united with one another in joy and radiance in the One Body of Christ.

THE SACRED TRADITION
(OIL-M:1386B)

23

12

THE GLORY OF HEAVEN.

Christ's true friends are all united 'in Him': His friends in Heaven and in Purgatory - and ourselves still labouring in earthly life.

Someone has knelt down to pray, apparently alone; but she knows that when she prays in the name of Christ, through the Spirit, to the Father in Heaven, she doesn't pray entirely alone before God.

We can be sure that our private words to God are really private; yet at the same time we can remember that we have a marvellous bond with everyone else who lives 'in Christ' in a state of grace. This is true no matter how bleak our circumstances - and however great our desire, perhaps, to remain separate from fellow human beings.

If we are spiritually alive as members of the living Body of Christ we are united in spirit with all the other members; and so we are united in prayer at every Mass, for example, first with the spiritual brothers and sisters we see around us, and also with the faithful people who have 'died in Christ' yet who are undergoing purification; and we are united in praise with the Saints of Heaven and with Christ our Saviour - and with all the Holy Angels who serve God and help His creatures.

From all Eternity, God has planned to gather together weak human beings who have been scattered by sin. The plan hasn't yet been brought to completion, but its triumph is certain; and meanwhile, generation after generation, Christ's faithful friends rise up to Heaven, where Christ and His Saints await them in Glory.

THE GLORY OF HEAVEN
(OIL-M:42A)

25

PART TWO

THE HOLY EUCHARIST

13

DIVINE LIFE, THROUGH BAPTISM.

*The newly-baptised person is full of Divine Life and glory,
and is freed from sin and made a member of the Church.*

Accompanied by a group of friends and relations, two faithful parents
have brought their child for baptism. That's why the child's guardian
Angel, who is radiant with the glory of Heaven, looks on with
tremendous joy.

Baptism is one of the Church's seven sacraments. These are effective
signs through which the life of God is given to us or increased. When
a child or an adult is baptised with water, "in the Name of the Father
and of the Son and of the Holy Spirit," that person receives the gift of
Divine life within the soul.

Though we detect no outward change, we know by faith that this
person is a 'new creature' whose sins have been forgiven - and who
has been made a member of the Church. This is an adopted child of
God, who can learn to call God: "Father", and who can be certain that
every sincere prayer is heard and answered.

Through Baptism, and later through Confirmation, we are enabled to
take our rightful place in the celebration of the Eucharist, one with
God's people in worship and praise.

DIVINE LIFE, THROUGH BAPTISM
(OIL-M:876)

29

14

THE WORD OF GOD.

*Christ the Word of God speaks to us
through the words of Holy Scripture.*

At every Mass, after the Penitential Rite, we celebrate the liturgy of the Word: and, after the first readings, we stand to hear the Holy Gospel. It is read to us by a member of the Clergy; yet it is Christ Who speaks to us, to teach and help us.

Christ is the Word of God; and He speaks to us today through Sacred Scripture, as well as through the Sacred Tradition of the Catholic Church, and through the Church's teaching authority. Whenever we listen with prayerful attention as the Gospel is read to us by a member of the Clergy we hear precisely those truths or reminders of truth which Christ wants to give each one of us at that moment.

Christ is the Son of God: the One Who shows us what the Father is like: the One Who makes visible the Father's loving-kindness, and Who speaks the truths we need to know if we sincerely want to live as God's children in a sinful world.

THE WORD OF GOD
(OIL-M:888B)

31

15

A TORRENT OF GRACES.

*As we praise God, it's as if He pours out a great torrent
of grace upon us, from His ever-open, loving 'heart'.*

It's as if a great torrent of grace is pouring upon us throughout the
Mass, from the ever-open, fiery, generous 'heart' of God the Father.
Though we cannot see Him we know that He loves us and that He
gives 'grace upon grace' to all who open their hearts to Him and
believe in His promises.

In every era of Christian history, men, women and children have
stood before God in adoration and joy, awed by the immensity of His
majesty and power yet confident that He will act on their behalf.

That's what He does in every Mass, when He sends His Holy Spirit to
our altar to effect an astonishing change in the gifts we've offered.
Yet in preparation for that moment, we say together the prayer which
begins: "Holy, holy, holy Lord, God of power and might. Heaven and
earth are full of Your Glory." As we do this, we are joining in the
praises of the holy Angels who worship beside us, the praises offered
to God by the Holy Souls who have gone before us, and the praises
being offered by the Saints and Angels in Heaven.

A TORRENT OF GRACES
(OIL-L:442A)

16

A WINDOW INTO TIME.

We who could not be with Christ on Calvary can be with Him today as He offers that same sacrifice at the hands of our priest.

At every Mass, it's as though we have been brought through a "window into time," to Calvary. We are standing at the foot of the Cross with Mary, Christ's Virgin Mother; and we can gaze upon the Person and the Act which have redeemed us.

At the heart of every Mass is the moment of Consecration, when, through the speech and actions of the priest, and the words of Christ which he utters, through the faith of the whole Church, and through the work of the Holy Spirit Who is powerfully at work in His Church, the bread and wine on the altar are changed into the Sacred Body and Precious Blood of Christ. In this way, the sacrifice of Christ on Calvary is re-presented before us.

The Mass is a memorial of the saving work of Christ on Calvary - and of His Resurrection and Ascension; yet it is a living memorial, not a mere remembrance, because Christ our Living Lord is Really Present amongst us, sacramentally; and indeed, He remains amongst us, in the Blessed Sacrament of the tabernacle.

Through His Infinite kindness, Christ has arranged that we who could not be with Him when He offered His life for us on Calvary can be with Him now, as He offers that same sacrifice at the hands of our priest.

A WINDOW INTO TIME
(OIL-L:59)

17

CHRIST OUR HIGH PRIEST.

*Christ is Really Present before us, 'whole and entire',
His body, blood, soul and divinity.*

It is by faith that we recognise Christ when we look upon the Sacred Host, after the Consecration. He is Really Present here: His Body, Blood, Soul and Divinity: the risen and glorified Son of God, Who loves to be amongst us. This is our High Priest, Who once sacrificed His life for our sakes. His sacrifice is re-presented at every Mass. It is here, at the Holy Sacrifice of the Mass, that the benefits of Christ's once-for-all sacrifice can be applied to us, and to our lives.

The glory of Heaven streams from Him, as He prays to the Father for our salvation. But even if we are awed by His goodness and generosity, we are at peace in our frailty.

Christ was called a 'friend of sinners', and so if we've seriously tried to change our lives with His help and to live in a state of grace, our sins forgiven, we are no longer made fearful at the thought of His holiness. We are not afraid to receive Him in Holy Communion.

CHRIST OUR HIGH PRIEST
(OIL-L:375)

37

18

THE ACCLAMATION.

*In our Acclamation, we express our faith in the Presence of
Christ our God, Whose unseen Glory fills our sanctuary.*

Here we see an image of the figure of Christ filling the sanctuary.
Christ is alive. He has risen from the dead, in triumph; so when His
Body and Blood are made present on the altar at the Consecration
Christ is not present with us in separate parts; rather, He is Present
'whole and entire', (CCC:1377) with His Body, Blood, and Soul and
Divinity: risen from the dead, and radiant with Heavenly glory.

Every Mass is a 'living memorial' of Christ's Paschal work, by which
we mean His suffering, His death, and His Resurrection and
Ascension; and now Christ can never die again.

Anyone who is amazed at the Father's marvellous gifts, or
overwhelmed at Christ's goodness in being amongst us in this special
manner, can cry out in wonder in the acclamation, before the priest
continues with the central prayer of the Church.

THE ACCLAMATION
(OIL-L:550)

39

19

WITH BANNERS UNFURLED.

*It's as if the banners of Heaven are waving as the
Saints and holy Angels join in our joyful praises
during our celebration of Christ's triumph over death.*

The joy of the Saints of Heaven, and of the holy Angels who are very close to us, never diminishes.

At every Mass, they are present with us in glory, though unheard and unseen. It's as if the banners of Heaven have been unfurled, in celebration of Christ's triumph over sin and death.

Every Mass is a living memorial of the death of Christ; yet at the same time it is a celebration of His Resurrection from the dead and His Ascension into Heaven: events which are so amazing and glorious and significant that it seems strange that we sometimes speak of them with little sign of gratitude and joy.

Yet a firm faith in Christ's triumph, with a sure hope of sharing Christ's Glory, for all Eternity, can help us to persevere in the dark times when our faith is weak or under attack; and by receiving Christ our God in Holy Communion, welcoming Him into our hearts and lives with sincere devotion, we can be made 'Godly' - by His Divine power and life and graces; and there are other wonderful benefits; for example, in receiving Christ we are bound ever closer to everyone else who is a member of His Body, the Church.

WITH BANNERS UNFURLED
(OIL-M:805)

41

20

IN SICKNESS AND FRAILTY.

Sick members of the Church need not be left without the comforting Presence of Christ. In receiving the Blessed Sacrament, they meet and receive Christ our loving God.

In the Holy Eucharist, Christ is Really Present - 'whole and entire' - bringing His Divine graces and His consoling friendship to those who love Him.

This is the marvel of the Real Presence of Christ in the Blessed Sacrament: that when a sick member of the Church is visited by the priest or the extraordinary minister of the Eucharist, that person receives what appears merely to be a wafer of unleavened bread; yet this is no longer bread, but the Body of Christ.

The sick person who receives Christ with faith and gladness is enabled to bear sufferings in greater patience and peace, and even to accept them, and 'offer them up' on behalf of other people in union with the Crucified Christ; and in this privileged manner, a suffering person can join in Christ's redeeming work.

Sometimes, through the presence of Christ and the response of faith, the sick person is strengthened and healed in mind, body or spirit.

IN SICKNESS AND FRAILTY
(OIL-M:1038B)

43

21

CHRIST AMONGST HIS PEOPLE.

Christ is amongst us, at the heart of the Church, at the centre of our lives - and in the midst of all our sufferings.

No matter how dark the times, we can know, by faith, that Christ is amongst us, leading us steadily towards Heaven - if we will stay close to Him and let Him illuminate our path.

Christ has promised to His followers: 'I will be with you always.' This is what His Church teaches us, through Holy Scripture, and this is what His faithful friends all know to be true.

Even if we cannot see Him with our bodily eyes or hear Him with our ears, we know that He speaks to us through His word, read out to us during the Liturgy. He is present wherever His Body, the Church - our spiritual brothers and sisters - is gathered in worship or service. He is present teaching and sanctifying us through our priests, who are 'icons' of Christ for us; and - most marvellous of all - we know that Christ is sacramentally Present with us when we gaze at the round white disc - the Sacred Host - held up high by the priest after the Consecration at Mass.

This is Christ, Really Present - for us to receive in Holy Communion, if we are in a state of grace. This is Christ, Really Present, for all to adore before the tabernacle.

CHRIST AMONGST HIS PEOPLE
(OIL-M:1327)

PART THREE

THE SPIRITUAL JOURNEY

22

IN THE NAME OF CHRIST.

*Even if we seem to be weak and powerless, we can
be sure that our prayers are powerful, because they
are offered in the Name of Christ our God, and Mediator.*

Even if we are weak and powerless, like the little person in the chair,
our prayers are gigantic, if we offer them to the Father in the Name of
Christ, and by the Spirit's power.

If we have really put our trust in Christ, we know that God the Father
sent His Son to die for us and to bring us back to His embrace; and we
know that through Baptism, we have become children of God:
brothers and sisters of Christ. We know that we can rely on the power
of Christ to bring grace from Heaven into our hearts and lives; and we
know that we can praise the Father worthily by praising Him with, in
and through Christ, Whose praise is always powerful and glorious: so
there's no need to worry about our human frailty.

Everything good we do in the Name of Christ is worthy of Heaven -
whether an act of kindness, a piece of work, a patient acceptance of
unavoidable suffering or a brief sincere prayer; and we have the joy of
knowing that Christ offers perpetual prayer on our behalf, as St. Paul
says - and the joy of knowing that the Father to Whom we pray is full
of love for us, and infinitely kind.

IN THE NAME OF CHRIST
(OIL-M:817)

49

23

THE LITTLEST PRAYER.

The littlest prayer to our Father in Heaven
is welcomed, heard, valued and rewarded.

Whenever we pray with real trust and humility we are very close to Heaven's 'border'. It's as though Heaven lies just above our heads: and 'Heaven is our homeland' (Phil 3:20): a place of light and sweetness and love.

Our Heavenly Father, Who is one with the Son and the Spirit, is always waiting as if at the edge of Heaven: waiting to listen to our prayers. He delights in the humility with which we approach Him, and in the trust which we demonstrate by our prayers. The littlest prayer, and the briefest whisper to God, is welcomed, heard, valued and rewarded. It's as though the Father is lovingly, tenderly stroking the neck of His own precious child, as He reaches out to caress each person who trusts in Him and confides every need.

As God's children, we have the sure knowledge that He loves us at every moment. We can turn to Him whenever we please, in trusting prayer: certain of being heard and answered.

Those who have been made children of God are sometimes tempted to imagine that God is 'absent', when the truth is that He is very close indeed, and is lovingly holding us in existence; yet we can increase our faith in Him by making an act of faith each time we begin our prayer. If we say, as we begin: "I believe that You are close to me. I believe that You love me" - we have opened wide the 'door' of our souls; and His spiritual light can shine in, to increase our hope and faith and love.

THE LITTLEST PRAYER
(OIL-M:1396)

51

24

THE ABYSS.

Someone who clings by faith to a thin thread of hope, in spiritual darkness, seems to be suspended above a deep Abyss.

There is a gulf which separates human beings from the Godhead: a gulf between the All-holy God Who lives on high in radiant splendour, and His sinful creatures, and this is a gulf which can only be crossed through and in Christ.

There are times in the life of every sincere follower of Christ when it seems as if the gulf is unbridgeable - or the way across uncertain; and in such times of darkness in prayer, or pain and turmoil in everyday life, the faithful soul might feel as though he has been left suspended above the dark void. He can't remain content with earthly pursuits; but he doesn't yet taste the joys of union with God. It's as though this soul, with an interior anguish which seems unending, and unendurable, clings by faith to a thin thread of hope.

Only through an unfelt yet pure love for God - and by God's grace - does such a soul avoid despair or danger, willing to bear this time of trial, believing that God can bring deliverance. But such a dark time can prove to be immensely worthwhile. If we have been made adopted children of God, through Christ, we have a sure hope of Heaven, if we remain faithful to the end; and throughout our journey towards the Kingdom we should remember that every sincere prayer which we offer through Christ to the Father, in the Spirit, is greeted with delight.

THE ABYSS
(OIL-M:472)

53

25

THE SOUL AS A CAVERN.

*If we enter within our own 'heart' in order to find God,
it's as though we rest within a cavern, to await Him.*

We can picture the interior of our soul as being like a cavern: a secret place which we can enter in order to find God. There, in silent attention to Him in humility and wonder, we wait for Him to reveal Himself; and, meanwhile, when we have cleared away some of the sin and clutter from our heart and life, Heaven's Light begins to shine within the soul.

Peace and joy in prayer are gifts from God, given to those who have prepared their hearts by prayer and penance and acts of charity, and by perseverance in faith through all sorts of trials and even persecutions.

Those whom God has drawn into a life of prayer and who cling to Him through His scorching purifications find, in the end, that Heaven's joys are incomparable: Heaven's joys 'tasted' even here in earthly life. No earthly love, no natural happiness, no worldly fulfilment nor any human joy can rival the joys given to the faithful soul in the intimacy of Divine Union.

THE SOUL AS A CAVERN
(OIL-M:350)

26

TO HEAVEN, IN CONTEMPLATION.

*God our Father greets with delight our
merest whisper of sincere prayer.*

God sometimes reaches 'down', as if to seize the faithful soul and to draw her briefly up to Heaven in contemplative prayer, to experience His love, radiance, and sweetness.

No-one can seize these gifts from God. He gives them when He chooses to those who give Him first place in their lives and who approach Him with reverence and love.

Prayer is a gift from God: a process or conversation which begins when we respond to God's prompting and open our hearts to Him, giving Him our full attention.

And when we are faithful to God in regular prayer, and in loving service of our neighbour, we allow God to act within our souls and lives.

When we have continued to share our inmost thoughts with God, to express sorrow for sins, to thank Him for His blessings, to praise and adore Him - with words and without - and to sit in attentive silence before Him, we allow Him to surprise us; and He does so, at last, by drawing the soul into union with Himself, in incomparable joy.

TO HEAVEN, IN CONTEMPLATION
(OIL-M:1406)

27

THE GOLDEN THREAD.

*Our daily duty is like a ball of string at our feet, and
a golden thread, by which we can follow God's Will,
confident of being on the path to Heaven.*

This string represents the duty that God asks us to fulfil each day.
Whoever asks questions about how to serve God can be certain that if
they will pick up the 'golden string' which God has left at their feet -
their everyday duty - they can please Him and become holy.

For generation after generation Christ has been teaching us, through
His Church, how to become holy; but despite such guidance, people
sometimes say: "I seem to live in uncertainty and darkness. I don't
see how I can do great things for God, because every avenue seems
closed to me; so how can I possibly please God?"

If, out of love for God, they follow the 'string', and faithfully carry
out their everyday duties, they can be certain that they are loving God
and loving their neighbour, and that they are making their way
steadily past all obstacles towards the Light of Heaven.

A further reason for not ignoring God's wishes in everyday matters is
that He has promised that great tasks are given only to people who
have been faithful in little ones.

THE GOLDEN THREAD
(OIL-M:1445)

28

LOVE FOR OUR NEIGHBOUR.

*Christ greets other people in a holy and happy way
through each tender word or gesture we offer.*

It is not enough for Christ's friends to listen to Christ's words in the Mass, to greet Christ lovingly at the Consecration, to offer His sacrifice to the Father, from the altar, and to receive Christ in Holy Communion.

As we leave the church at the end of Mass to immerse ourselves again in everyday work or domestic life, we cannot keep to ourselves the Divine graces which have been poured within our souls through our communion with Heaven. We cannot savour them only as personal gifts from God to ourselves. He wants us to share our joy, and our good news.

If we are real friends of Christ, and have allowed Him to transform us, through the Sacred Liturgy, we can go out to share Christ's love and peace and joy, bringing them as personal gifts from Christ to each person we meet in the days and weeks ahead.

LOVE FOR OUR NEIGHBOUR
(OIL-M:651)

29

AN OPEN HEART.

*A person full of God's love carries in her heart a triple
fire of love, in which she 'holds' all the needy.*

Whoever claims to love God sincerely must love the people whom
God has made. If we hold within our hearts our families and friends,
and the people we meet in everyday life - and especially people in
need - we shall begin to act as Christ acted on earth.

We shall listen to others, serve them, hold them before God in prayer,
share their heartache, pray for them during and after their death, and
strive to be worthy to join them in Heaven, we hope, when we die, our
hearts full of Christ's Light and charity.

The fire of Divine love which has filled our hearts on earth will be our
glory when we enter Heaven.

AN OPEN HEART
(OIL-M:565)

30

POWERFUL ASSISTANCE.

By one prayer, offered in Christ's name, we can support hundreds of people in need, strengthening them by His grace and kindness.

To intercede for other people in the Name of Christ is to hold out a hand to someone in need and to be confident of giving support. We know that the support we give to someone else depends on the support Christ gives to us - as he stands 'behind' us. In praying for one person, we might be helping a hundred, all of whom are dependent upon the person we are praying for.

Our desire to help other people through prayer is increased if we realise how much we all depend upon one another for such brief moments of support - or even for life changing or life saving intervention.

Through prayer in Christ's Name, we can bring about powerful changes in peoples' lives, drawing Divine graces upon someone who is perhaps undergoing a trial of faith: or to someone uncertain about a vocation, or approaching despair about weaknesses and temptations.

And if there are people in need of food or shelter, whom we can't reach with practical help, it's still worth praying. We can ask God to steer towards them people who will alleviate their sufferings.

POWERFUL ASSISTANCE
(OIL-M:1108)

65

31

LEANING ON THE CROSS.

*In all our sufferings we can reach out in spirit, to lean on
the Cross and to unite our sufferings with those of Christ.*

When the Christian way of life seems fruitless, or when the effort to
love seems impossible to sustain, or our sufferings too great to bear,
we need not recite insincere words in prayer. We can simply place
ourselves in spirit beside the God-man who has suffered and died for
us. We can 'lean' on the Cross and unite our sufferings with those of
Christ.

It shouldn't surprise us to find that, in our communion with Heaven,
we experience desolation as well as consolation. It is a life-long task
we undertake as we strive to be 'conformed to Christ' by loving God
with our whole heart and mind and strength, and loving our neighbour
for God's sake.

Yet we who pray to God the Father in the Name of Christ can be
confident that the Holy Spirit is at work within us and that the Father
hears our prayers.

If we are willing to share Christ's suffering we can even share in His
redeeming work - and we have a sure hope of sharing His
Resurrection; and these thoughts can comfort us, when all we're
aware of is pain and darkness.

LEANING ON THE CROSS
(OIL-M:104)

32

THE COMMUNION OF SAINTS.

The Saints in Heaven are alive, and very close to us. They love
to hear us speak to them; and they respond to our requests.

Every Christian believer is encouraged by the awareness that a cloud
of witnesses in Heaven spurs us on as we make our way towards our
true homeland. The Saints who live in glory are very close to us; yet
they are not mere onlookers. Nor are they merely models of holiness.

Though we can't see them, we are in communion with them, through
our relationship with Christ. They love to hear our greetings, and our
requests for prayer. They are very pleased to see us share and
celebrate their feast-days; and when they turn to God to intercede for
us they bring down God's blessings upon us.

So, if we are 'one' with them, in the Church, it's only sensible to try
to know them better, to speak to them, to celebrate their feast days
with joy, and to study their lives. We can learn from their example
that no cross is unbearable, no obstacle unsurmountable, if we put our
whole trust in Christ and in the gifts and graces which He pours into
every contrite and trusting heart.

We can also learn that real earthly joys pale into insignificance when
compared with the joys of Divine union.

THE COMMUNION OF SAINTS
(OIL-M:812B)

33

CLOSER TO THE LIGHT.

*The Holy Souls in Purgatory are advancing towards
Heaven's Light, helped by our prayers.*

All who have died 'in Christ' but who are not yet ready to enter
Heaven are held by God's love, in Purgatory. They are glad to be
able to undergo purification; but whether they experience the fire of
remorse on seeing their sins in God's clear light, or burn with
yearning to see the face of God, Whom they are not yet fit to see, they
are content with their state.

These Holy Souls are safe in God's merciful care, all earthly dangers
and temptations left behind.

They move closer and closer to the Glory of Heaven, awaiting the
moment when the holy Angels invite them to step forward. Then,
they can meet and greet, in a moment of utter bliss and fulfilment and
Heavenly radiance, the Three Divine Persons - One God - Who have
brought them through every earthly trial to enter the Heavenly
homeland.

CLOSER TO THE LIGHT
(OIL-M:516)

34

THE HOLY TRINITY.

Christ is holding out His hand, inviting each one of us to step forward to share His Divine life at the heart of the Holy Trinity.

Christ reigns in Heaven, in Glory, with the Father and the Holy Spirit, in the unity of the Godhead. Christ is God-made-man. He really died on the Cross, and then rose from the grave to new life. He can never die again. He is now in Heaven, where He holds out His wounded hand to welcome each person who approaches Him in love and humility. This is the Saviour who endured torment on earth because of His longing to save us; and He is eternally the Priest and Mediator for His earthly brothers and sisters. We are very precious to Him. In the depths of our prayer therefore, and even in the apparent tragedy of the moment of our death, Christ welcomes us, His true friends, to the heart of the Holy Trinity.

In the wondrous life of Heaven, the holy and majestic Father, Who eternally embraces His Divine Son and the Holy Spirit, sees and knows everything which exists through Him, and sees and knows everyone He has created. He calls all people towards Himself, to live in His love.

Here, in God's holy light, the Holy Spirit - Divine love and eternal source of joy - is endlessly loving the happy souls whom He has been drawing towards the Godhead. He now holds them in His tender embrace for evermore. All their sufferings ended, they now experience the incomparable, indescribable bliss of union with God in Eternal life, at the heart of the Holy Trinity.

THE HOLY TRINITY
(OIL-M:1039C)

A SUMMARY OF OUR CHRISTIAN STORY: FROM HOLY SCRIPTURE.

"At various times in the past and in various different ways, God spoke to our ancestors through the prophets; but in our own time, the last days, he has spoken to us through his Son, the Son that he has appointed to inherit everything and through whom he made everything there is. He is the radiant light of God's glory and the perfect copy of his nature, sustaining the universe by his powerful command; and now that he has destroyed the defilement of sin, he has gone to take his place in heaven at the right hand of divine Majesty. So he is now as far above the angels as the title which he has inherited is higher than their own name." (Heb 1: 1-4)

"Since in Jesus, the Son of God, we have the supreme high priest who has gone through to the highest heaven, we must never let go of the faith that we have professed. For it is not as if we had a high priest who was incapable of feeling our weaknesses with us; but we have one who has been tempted in every way that we are, though he is without sin. Let us be confident, then, in approaching the throne of grace, that we shall have mercy from him and find grace when we are in need of help." (Heb 4:14-16)

"During his life on earth, he offered up prayer and entreaty, aloud and in silent tears, to the one who had the power to save him out of death, and he submitted so humbly that his prayer was heard. Although he was Son, he learnt to obey through suffering; but having been made perfect, he became for all who obey him the source of eternal salvation." ... (Heb 5:7-9).

"But you, my dear people - in spite of what we have just said, we are sure you are in a better state and on the way to salvation. God would not be so unjust as to forget all you have done, the love that you have for his name or the services you have done, and are still doing, for the saints. Our one desire is that every one of you should go on showing the same earnestness to the end, to the perfect fulfilment of our hopes, never growing careless, but imitating those who have the faith and the perseverance to inherit the promises." (Heb 6:9-12)

*****

What is Radiant Light?

Radiant Light is a small movement within the Roman Catholic Church which seeks to encourage people to grow in faith and to share their faith with others. The movement was founded by Elizabeth Wang - a Catholic housewife, mother and artist - in obedience to the wishes of Christ, Who is 'the radiant light of God's Glory' (Heb 1:3). She has received many teachings and visions from him to renew the Church, and over the last few years she has been writing, painting and talking about them. These teachings are simply reminders of the constant teaching of the Church, centred on Christ and his presence in the Holy Eucharist. Radiant Light is also a small non-profit-making company which publishes the works of Elizabeth Wang and organises various events about the Catholic Faith.

It has wide trading objects, together with two specific aims which are:

> *'For the glory of God the Most Holy Trinity, for the honour of the Blessed Virgin Mary, and out of love for the Catholic Church and loyalty to the Pope and the bishops in communion with him'*

(1) to advance the Roman Catholic religion
(2) to promote the works of Elizabeth Wang

Please write to the Harpenden address below if you would like to be put on the mailing list.

If you would like to help support the work of Radiant Light, please send a UK cheque to **Radiant Light, 25 Rothamsted Avenue, Harpenden, Herts, AL5 2DN., U.K.** Cheques must be made payable to 'Radiant Light'. Thank you.

Company No. 3701357 (Company limited to guarantee and not having a share capital).

Visit the Radiant Light web-site at:
www.radiantlight.org.uk

Book Orders and Distribution.

Radiant Light books, photographs and posters are available from St. Pauls book shop next to Westminster Cathedral, London:

**St. Pauls
(By Westminster Cathedral)
Morpeth Terrace
Victoria
London SW1P 1EP
United Kingdom.**

**Tel: 020 7828 5582
Fax: 020 7828 3329**

email: bookshop@stpauls.org.uk

Mail-Order: If you would like to order Radiant Light works through the post, St Pauls has a very efficient *mail-order service,* which will send your order throughout the UK and anywhere in the world. Please telephone St Pauls and ask them how you may order Radiant Light books. *But please do not send money or orders until you have been in touch with them.*